The Nuffield St

GW01561220

"NUFFIELD TO MAKE TRACTORS" was the announcement made by Sir Miles Thomas, vice-chairman of the Nuffield Organisation when he spoke to the I.S.M.A. at Hull in late March 1946. The tractor would have been 30% more power and be 30% sturdier than the average tractor available due to the involvement in its design by Mr Claude Culpin and Dr H. E. Merrif, who was well known for his part in tank design during the war.

The tractor was to be called the Nuffield Universal and was intended to be an all round farm machine with a high level of specification and fitments. Within two months the first prototype tractor was being field tested in Lincolnshire and by the end of the summer another dozen machines were being used for performance reports prior to a demonstration of three and four wheeled tractors at Pershore in late 1946.

It was fully intended to proceed with production in a big way in 1947, but due to material shortages this was not possible. However, the design team was kept hard at work improving the tractor and fitments, this included a completely new hydraulic lift.

By 1948 materials became available to the Nuffield Organisation to start tractor production with a stipulation by the Government that the first 12 months production be sold in the UK market to help produce home-grown foodstuffs after the war years.

Introduced at the Smithfield Show, in December 1948, the new 'Nuffield Universal' production models were a deal bigger than the prototypes and also sported revised tinwork and the new hydraulic lift, built at the old Wolseley factory in Birmingham. The tractors were painted poppy orange, and black engine accessories; priced at £487 for the basic M3 (three wheeler) and £495 for the M4 (four wheeler).

Listed as extras were the hydraulic lift and PTO unit at £60, belt pulley £12, and electric lights £9.

The tractors used a Morris Commercial ETA (M4) and ETB (PM4) four cylinder side valve engine (which had been originally designed for army use). Running on vaporising oil, the HP developed at 2000rpm was 38. The manifold was fitted with a heat shield and incorporated an adjustable hot spot operated by an external control; a lever operated radiator shutter gave accurate temperature control and the fuel system had independent cocks and sediment bowls.

By late 1950 the 2000th Nuffield Universal tractor had been exported by Nuffield Exports Ltd., to such countries as: Australia, New Zealand, Sweden, Holland, Denmark, Eire and Egypt; a shipment was due to go to Argentina early in 1951 and it was expected that an order would be despatched to the Belgian Congo which would be an entirely new market for British tractors.

1950 saw the introduction of the diesel engined Nuffield tractor which used the proven Perkins P4; this model was bought out to extend the range to three models available in three or four wheel form priced at £490 for a basic M4 to £667.10s0d (£667.50) for the high spec DM4. Standard equipment included electric starting, canvas cover and swinging, adjustable drawbar. Optional equipment included hydraulic power unit, belt pulley, electric lighting, wheel weights, etc.

In 1952 the British Motor Corporation was formed by the merger of Austin and Morris, and the tractors were produced by Morris Motors Ltd., Agricultural Division, Birmingham. A redesigned engine 'ETC' which raised the bhp to 43 was introduced in March/April 1953. This had improved combustion chambers, the cylinder head had long reach 14mm plugs, and ignition was by coil and distributor; the engine lubrication system was also improved and by moving the starting dog to the snout of the crankshaft the starting handle could be used even if the front end weight was fitted. Other changes in the model at this time were the fitting of a mid-mounted drawbar, and the replacement of t[...] [...]by two wheels mounted close together on the steering pillar and sharply cambered, the tractor serial numbers with these changes started at 11954 (M4) and 75860 (PM4) but the basic price remained unchanged at £465 for the M4.

By March 1954, a new diesel engine designed and manufactured by BMC was available and Nuffield tractors with this unit were first seen at the Royal Highland Show in June. The OEA2 engine was a four cylinder direct injection type with bore and stroke of 95mm and 120mm respectively; capacity was 3402cc and it was claimed to be 10% more economical on fuel than the P4 that it replaced. Power at the flywheel was 45bhp, other features were the five bearing counter — balanced crankshaft, replaceable wet cylinder liners, Lucas 12-volt starting equipment and Simms fuel injection. Induction and exhaust manifolds were mounted on opposite sides of the engine with air cleaner pre-cleaner mounted under the bonnet. These tractors were also called model DM and the price for the basic model remained at £597.10s0d (£597.50), ex works.

Also in 1954, the hydraulic lift pump was increased from 1000psi to 2000psi working pressure. The serial number position for the hydraulic power unit was stamped on the cross shaft housing next to the valve adjusting screws, and the early units which had BSF type threads ended at no. 17979. This was superceded by the unit using unified threads at no. 17980 and the new 2000lbs unit began at 2000/U001. Further improvements to the DM were the fitting of an improved oil filler which extended through the bonnet top, an independent PTO which was listed as an additional extra on new tractors only.

In 1957 a smaller tractor was added to the range, the Universal Three which used a 3 cylinder version of the 3.4 litre BMC diesel. It was a bit cumbersome compared with other models at the lower end of the market and did not become as popular as equivalent Ford or MF models. The DM4 became the Universal Four at the same time and the only outward change in appearance was the lack of sliding rear hubs which up until then had been a standard fitting. By 1957/58 the PM series tracters were only produced for export and the M4 was slowly being phased out due to the popularity of the diesel engine.

Production was then moved to the Morris factory at Cowley, near Oxford; consequently two new tractors were announced in November 1961 in time for the Royal Smithfield Show as the Nuffield 3/42 and 4/60. The 4/60 used a BMC 3.8 litre engine, producing 60bhp at 2000rpm, but still retained the five speed gearbox of the original DM4 series, whilst most competitors were offering a dual range 6-forward and 2-reverse transmission.

Another factory move was made in 1963, this time to Bathgate, in Scotland, where a new £11¼ million automatic assembly plant had been built and both engines and transmissions were made there along with BMC trucks. The following year both models were revised again, to become the 10/42 and the 10/60, so called because they now offered 10 forward and 2 reverse gears.

These two tractors were also fitted with an improved independent dual-flow hydraulic system, disc brakes and twin headlamps. Both tractors were offered in either basic, standard, or deluxe form, and a range of optional equipment was available.

In 1965 BMC announced their new lightweight mini-tractor as a new era in power farming 'mini mechanisation'. Designed to be used round the farms for smaller jobs it used a 950cc diesel engine, nine forward and reverse motion. This small tractor had its ancestry in the TE Ferguson, and had the hydraulic power unit mounted above the engine, and the oil tank was located under the driving seat for easy refuelling. Colour scheme was Nuffield orange, with white wheels and grille panel.

The last of the Nuffield range was introduced in 1967 at the Royal Show as the 3/45 and 4/65 models, available to basic, standard or deluxe specifications. Designed with the driver's needs in mind, the 3/45 and 4/65 models had an extended mainframe to carry the 15 gallon fuel tank forward of the engine; wide mudwings and footplates were also fitted along with a comprehensive range of instruments housed in a weatherproof panel. For easy access the engine cover could be raised without having to remove the exhaust pipe and for the first time ever, a Nuffield tractor was fitted with radius rods as standard.

Mechanically, these tractors were very much the same as the ones they had replaced, with a 3770cc four cylinder engine in the 4/65 and a 2827cc three cylinder in the 3/45. In November 1968 the 'mini tractor' was updated and fitted with a larger 1489cc engine and was known as the 4/25.

In 1968 BMC were taken over by Leyland and at the Royal Show that year, Lord Stokes, chairman of BLMC announced that the Nuffield tractor would be retained and developed under his re-organisation of BLMC. A new design team was set up at Bathgate to work on the tractor project and a year later the new models were announced as the 'Blue Range of Leyland'.

Sadly, after nearly a quarter of a century, the Nuffield name was dropped in favour of the famous truck and bus 'Leyland' badge, and the orange and white colour scheme gave way to two-tone blue, and silver on the new 384, 344 and 154 models. These new tractors did not change much from the Nuffields they replaced, apart from styling, and the 344 used a four cylinder 3402cc engine instead of a three cylinder type in the 3/45. The 154 was identical to the 4/25

and a petrol engine was available as an option.

From 1970 the Leyland tractor range was increased in many ways and improvements to such items as cabs, hydraulics, four wheel drive and turbo charged engines, and by December 1980 they had a range of 10 models on offer. December 1980 saw the introduction of a new range of models and a new yellow/black colour scheme on the 2 and 4 wheel drive tractors, but the 285 and 2100 models were dropped.

In 1981, Charles Nickerson, who owned Track Marshall floated a company to purchase the Leyland wheeled tractor division from Bathgate and proceeded to move all production machinery and stock to Gainsborough, where the tractors were to be produced by a new company: Marshall Sons & Company Ltd., when the tractors appeared under the slogan 'made better by Marshall', the specification remained the same as the previous models, but the Marshall formula was used to make existing features even better. Smithfield 1982 saw the name Marshall in place of Leyland, but the model's numbers remained unchanged with tractors ranging from 30 to 80 bhp.

By 1983 Marshall were obviously losing out on the higher horsepower market, so, using German ZF transmissions, 100 and 115HP tractors were added to the range, using Leyland engines. It had been hoped to move production of Leyland tractor engines to Gainsborough.

Prospects looked good for Marshall, but, in 1985 the company went into receivership. The track Marshall concern stayed put in a part of the works at Gainsborough following a management buyout, whilst the wheeled tractor side passed to Bentall Simplex, who moved stocks to Scunthorpe. A complete range of tractors are now offered, mainly built using imported components, and Perkins engines.

This is an artist's impression of what the Nuffield tractor would look like. Prototypes certainly differed in style from production units.

A prototype at work near Pershore in late 1946.

Above: The M4 with its rounded lines was to set the style for other manufacturer's products in the fifties. This is an early example with full specification, including pulley, lights, and hydraulic lift unit.

Above: The M4 in section. High clearance and a virtually direct drive line was achieved by mounting the bull pinion shafts above the rear axle, a feature which subequent models retained to the end of Marshall-Gainsborough production in 1985. Note the excellent ground clearance.

Above: The M3 featured a single front wheel and the method of fitting enabled a normal four wheeled tractor to be converted with ease. This is why the starting handle on early M4 tractors was offset. The reason for the small plate on the RH front of the radiator cowl can be seen here – its' removal allowed for the steering arm to be located to operate the single front wheel. Note the 9'' rear tyres. The front coverer is by Leverton. Nuffield did not make implements but issued a list of approved and tested implements made by leading manufacturers; most of these used carried an approved 'Nuffield Implement' badge if sold through Nuffield distributors.

Below: The DM4 required the use of the aircleaner in a forward position, to give room, under the bonnet, for the larger batteries needed to start the Perkins diesel. Even so, the bonnet side cover is larger.

Above: The DM4 used the Perkins P4 (TA) engine to bring a diesel option to the Nuffield range. The engine is seen to the right. This developed 39.6bhp at 2000rpm and was becoming popular in agriculture due to its low running costs. In 1950 a basic M4 cost £490 against £667 for a DM4.

Below: The Nuffield DM4 shows off its Rowcrop capability with special axle extensions.

Opposite page Above: A nearside view of a DM tractor with pan type wheels, new chaff screens, and BMC badge on the grille.

Opposite page Below: Introduced in August 1957 along with the Universal 3 the Universal 4 was advertised as "Up to the toughest job" . . . with down to earth economy". By this time the sliding rear hub was an optional extra and standard Sankey wheel centres were used.

Above: Introduced at serial number DE1001 the BMC engined tractors were still called model DMs. This is a fairly early example as can be seen from the type of steering, note also the engine cover with increased battery box and the position of the aircleaner. This model ended at No. DE10387.

Below: DM fitted with Roadless DG Half Tracks and front mounted weight. The tractor could not be fitted with hydraulics due to the idlers projecting outwith the limits of the rubber tyred units.

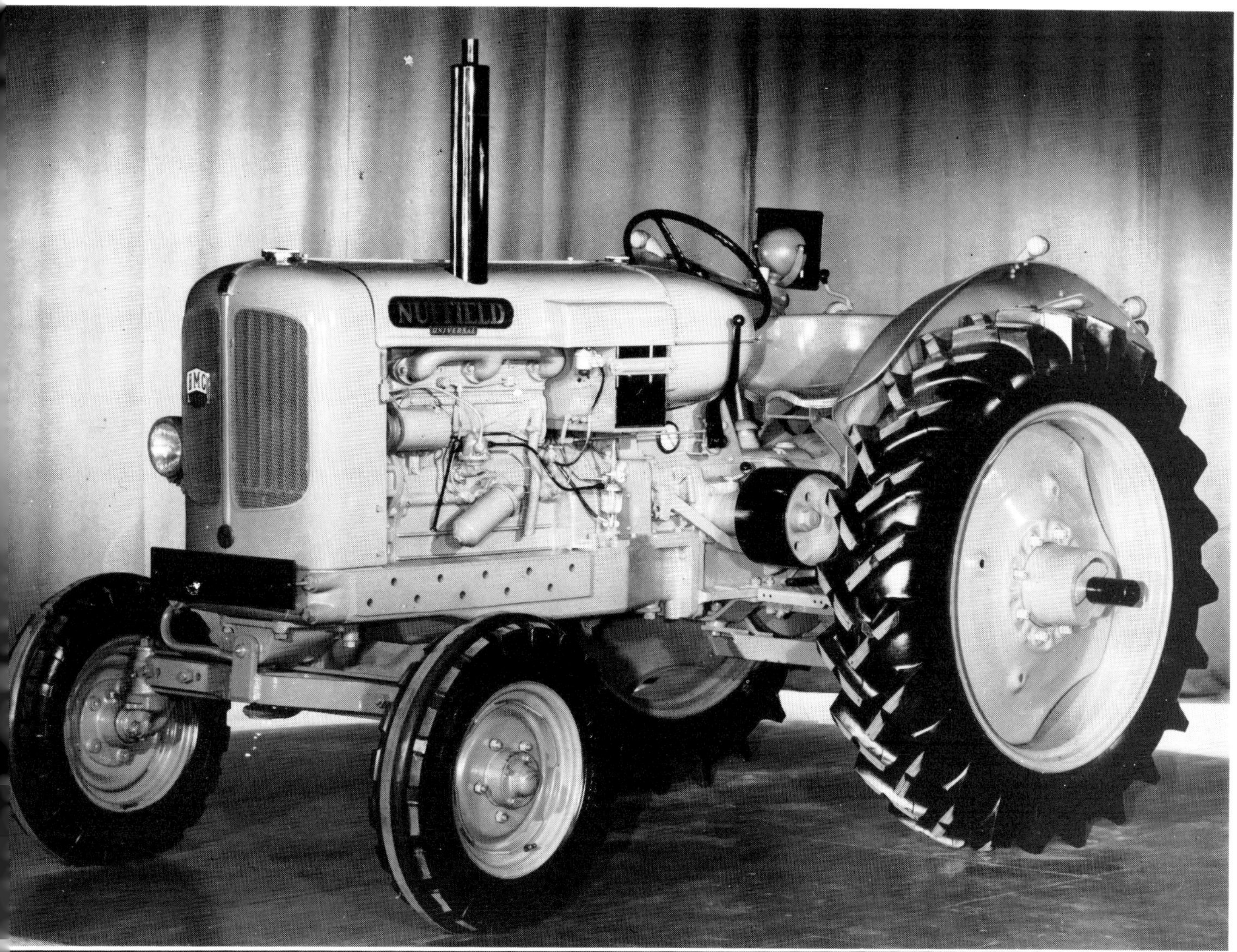
NUFFIELD
UNIVERSAL

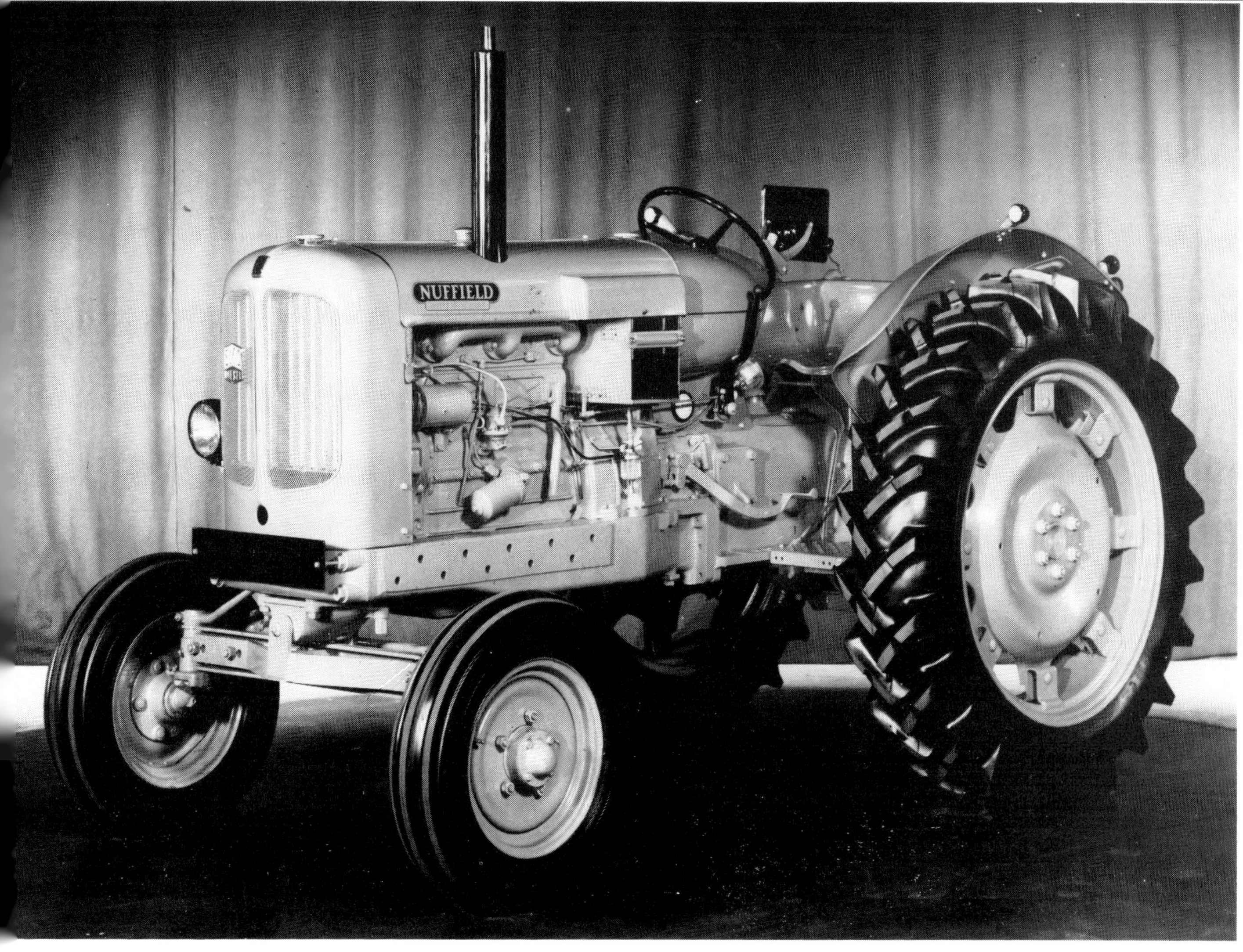
NUFFIELD

A Universal 4 with air pipe extension for overseas conditions.

Below: The Prototype 4WD Nuffield with power steering and Austin/Morris driving axle. Unfortunately this model did not go into production.

The new Universal 3 37bhp tractor was introduced in August 1957; built to compete with the MF35 and Fordson Dexta, the prototype machine used a cut and welded 3-cylinder engine made from an OEA/2 unit and was painted green for field testing.

Many parts for the Universal 3 were interchangeable with the larger Universal 4 making it rather a heavy tractor for its size. Standard wheel equipment was 5.50x16 fronts and 10.28 rears with a centre disc to rim adjustment as sliding hubs were not available on this model. The wheel equipment resulted in the 3 being 5" less in height than the 4, and it was only made in four wheel form.

A Universal 3 at work with Bamfords Forage harvester. The basic tractor would have cost £555.

This tractor appears to be a late Universal 4, but is, in fact, the prototype 4/60.

The 4/60 was introduced in December 1961 along with the 3 cylinder 3/42. These models replaced the Universal 4 and 3 and for the first time since 1946 the UNIVERSAL name was dropped.

The same 5-speed gearbox was retained on this model, but the engine power was increased to 60bhp. This probably made the 4/60 just about the most powerful tractor available at that time but it was lacking in gears, compared with its competitors.

Built until September 1964 the 3/42 and 4/60 were discontinued to make way for the Bathgate built 10/60 and 3/45s. The early example seen below shows the new style badges and provision for two headlamps.

Above: A 4/60 fitted with Sankey rear wheels and Lucas torque convertor (note the Lucas decals!).

The 10/60 engine, with its Simms' 'Minimec' pump is seen to the left.

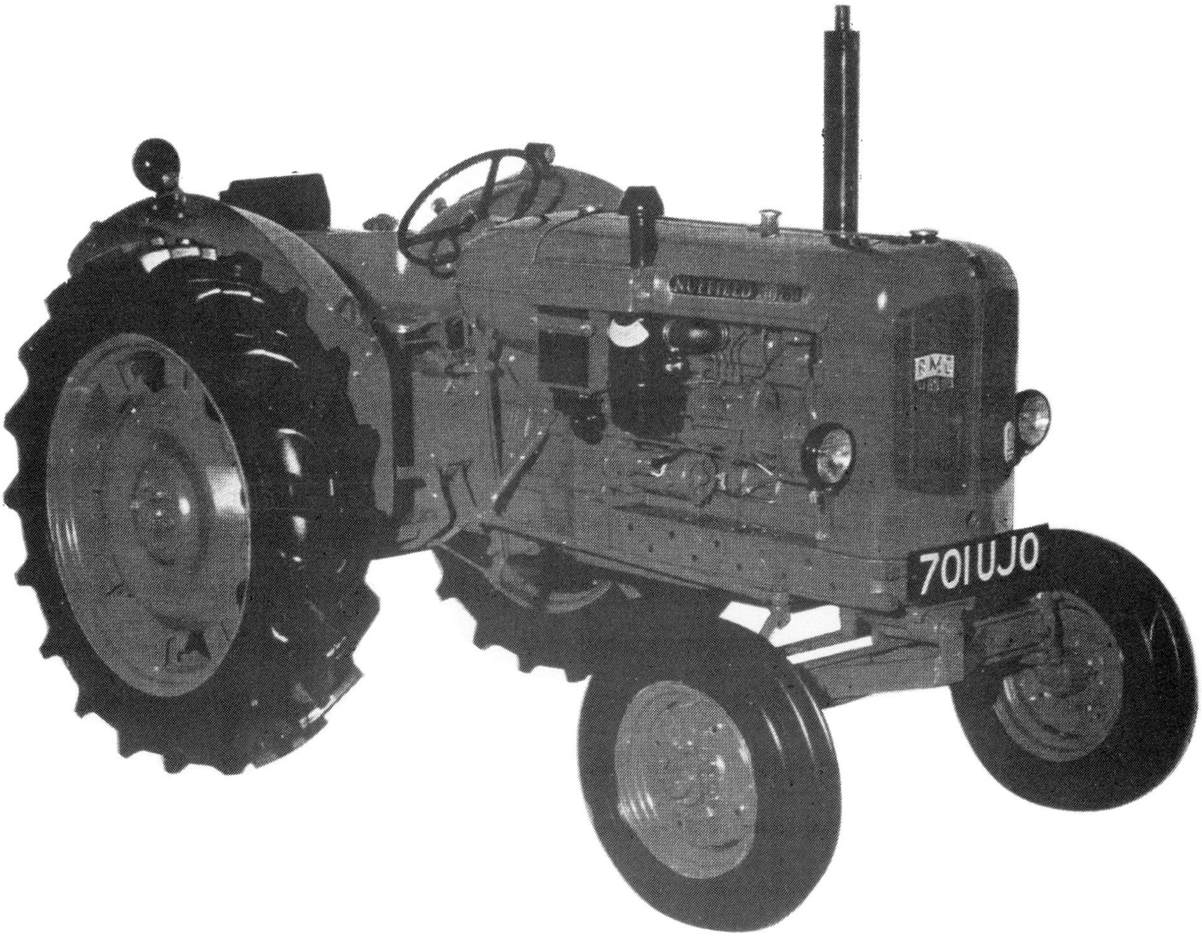
701UJO

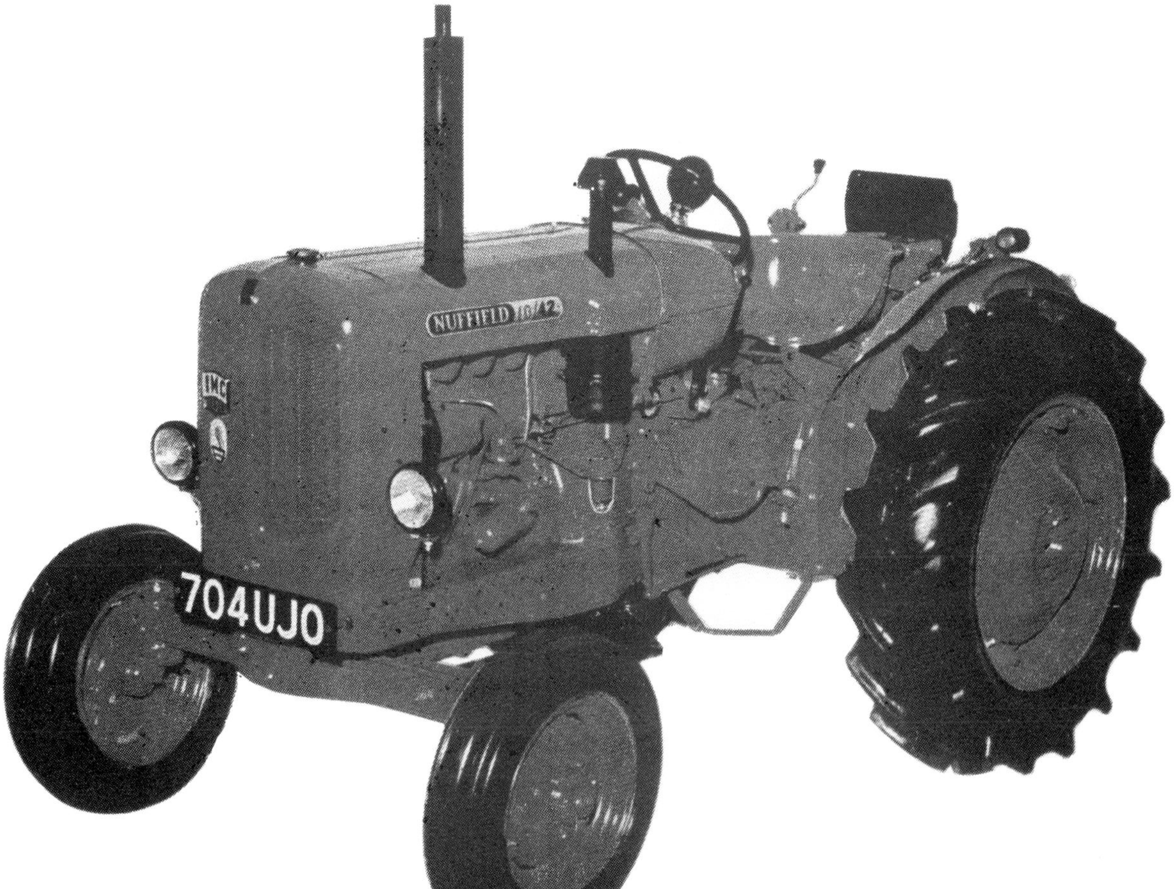
NUFFIELD 10/42
704UJO

The 10/60 (opposite upper) and 10/42 (opposite lower) were similar in appearance to their predecessors but had a new gearbox giving 10 forward speeds with the high and low range lever being mounted on the left hand side of a restyled instrument panel. Hydraulics were also improved, and detachable ball ends fitted to allow for category I or II implements. Disc brakes were also now standard.

Right: An export model 10/42. radius rods were fitted to these tractors but were still optional on the home market.

Left: An export model 10/60. These tractors offered additional optional extras such as six blade fan, heavy duty 13" clutch, and 5th speed excluder to cut down speed.

A 10/60 at work, possibly at Mosside Farm, Bathgate. Note the different lighting equipment used at the time, also the crimped silencer top – a BMC hallmark. Bray Construction also converted this model to give a Bray-Four 10/60.

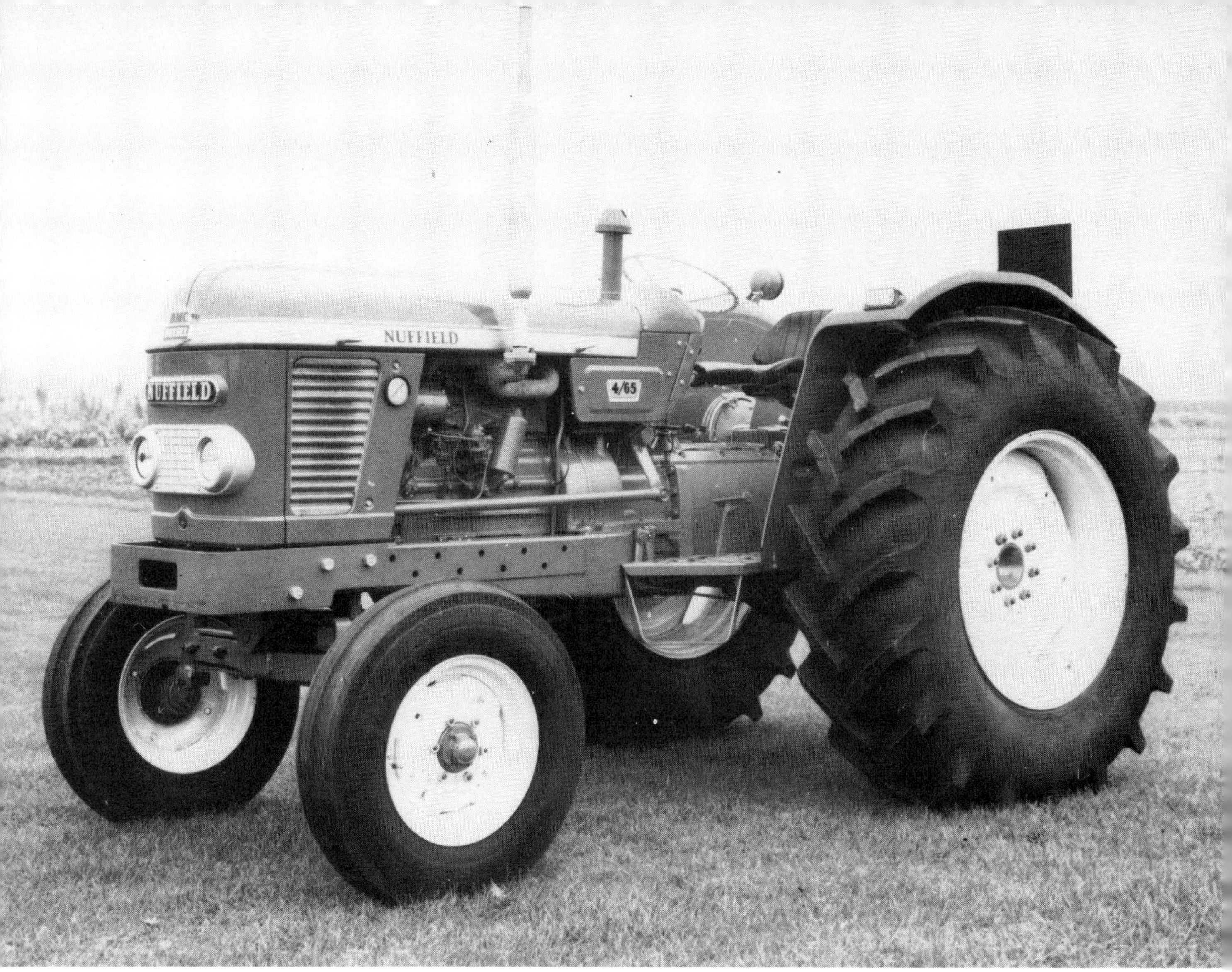
NUFFIELD
NUFFIELD
4/65

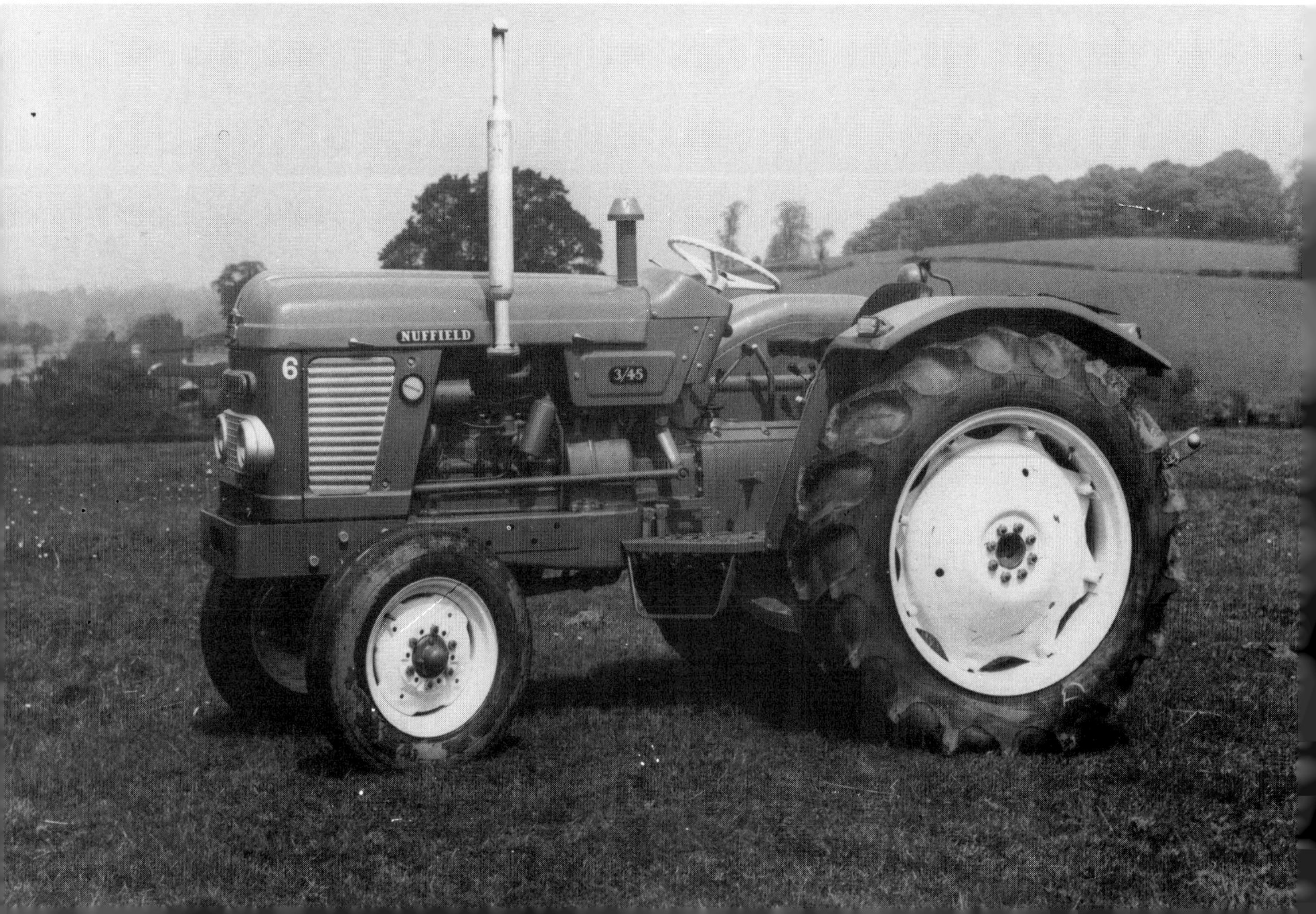
NUFFIELD
6
3/45

Out in time for The Royal Show, in July 1967, the new 4/65 (opposite upper) and 3/45 (opposite lower) models were the last of the true Nuffields.

New features included wide heavy type mudguards, front mounted fuel tank, steering drag link incorporated inside the engine mounting frame, improved positioning of hydraulic levers and new draught control with a two way sensitive top link valve giving uniform work at all settings. This feature was only possible due to the expiration of Ferguson patents, but it took longer for Nuffield to adopt draft control than other manufacturers.

The colour scheme for the tractors was still poppy orange, but the wheel centre, side panel inserts, and headlight mounting/grill unit were white. The view above shows a 4/65 with a Bamfords 'Wizzler' mower at The Royal Show in 1967. All of the components on the mower had been costed by one of the authors (ATC), who worked at Bamfords at that time.

A 4/65 is seen below with Steelfab loader.

The revolutionary "new from the ground, up" BMC Mini Tractor, was available from 1st December 1965. Planned round the driver this small tractor, which was developed by a specialist engineering design team over a six year period, boasted Britain's smallest volume produced diesel engine of 948cc, derived from the proven BMC 'A' series petrol engine. Gearing was through a new constant mesh gearbox giving nine forward and three reverse gears arranged in four speed ratios, low, medium, high, and reverse. Independent disc brakes were fitted and used a three pedal arrangement for field and road work.

Unfortunately, the MINI-TRACTOR did not sell well as it was underpowered and on the small size for most farm jobs dispite a range of implements being available from manufacturers such as Bamford, Teagle, and Salopian.

Above: In an attempt to increase sales, the BMC-mini was restyled to the Nuffield 4/25 in November 1968, and was now fitted with a BMC 1.5L diesel engine. The wheels were now painted white to match the larger Nuffields.

Left: Conveniently arranged controls of the 4/25. Note the three brake pedals, fuel tank mounted under the seat, and rear number plate which could be hinged down to clear the lift arms when in work.

Below: A 4/25 at work with two furrow plough. Bottom: Another view of the 4/25 cultivating, showing the nearside of the tractor.

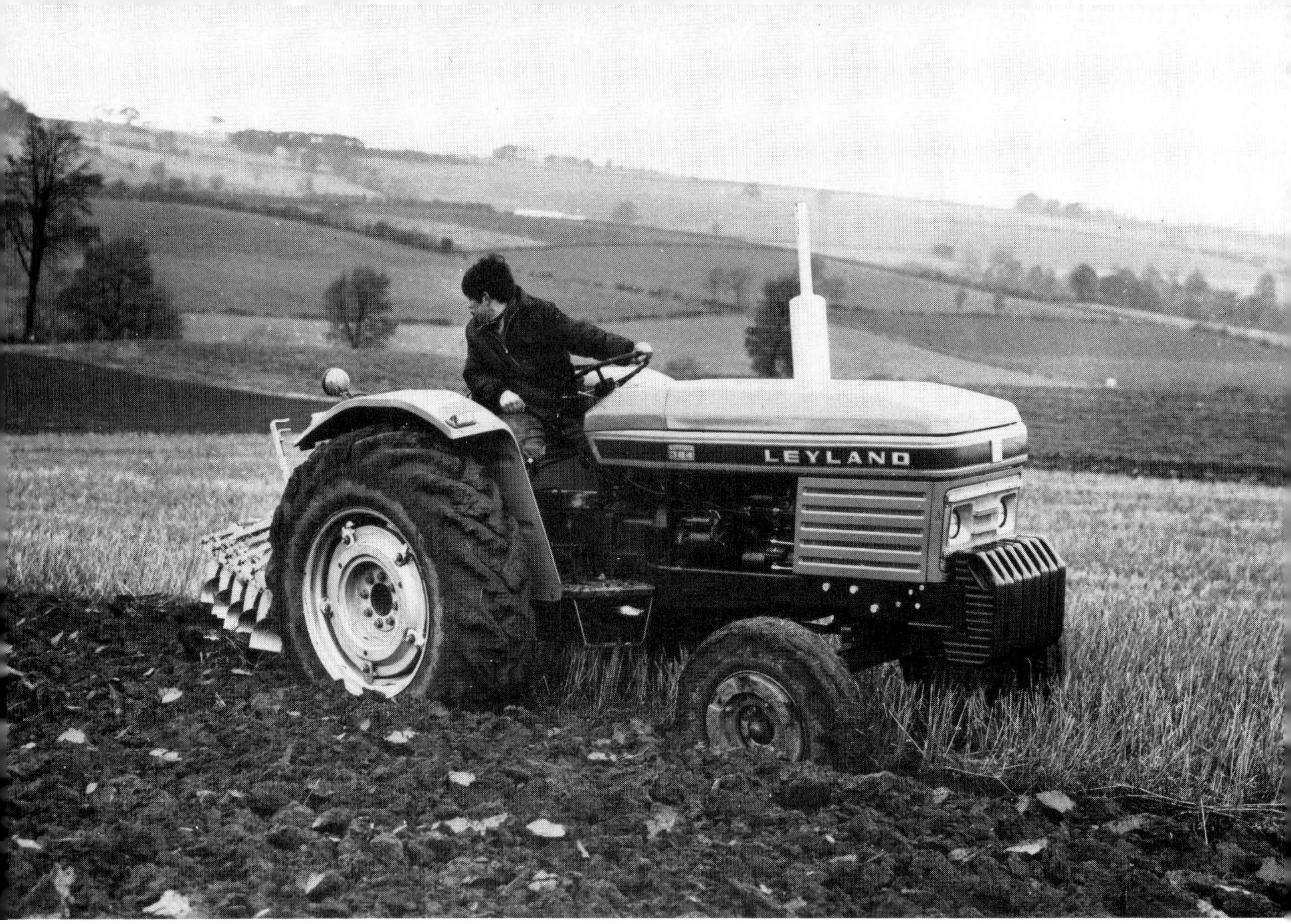
LEYLAND

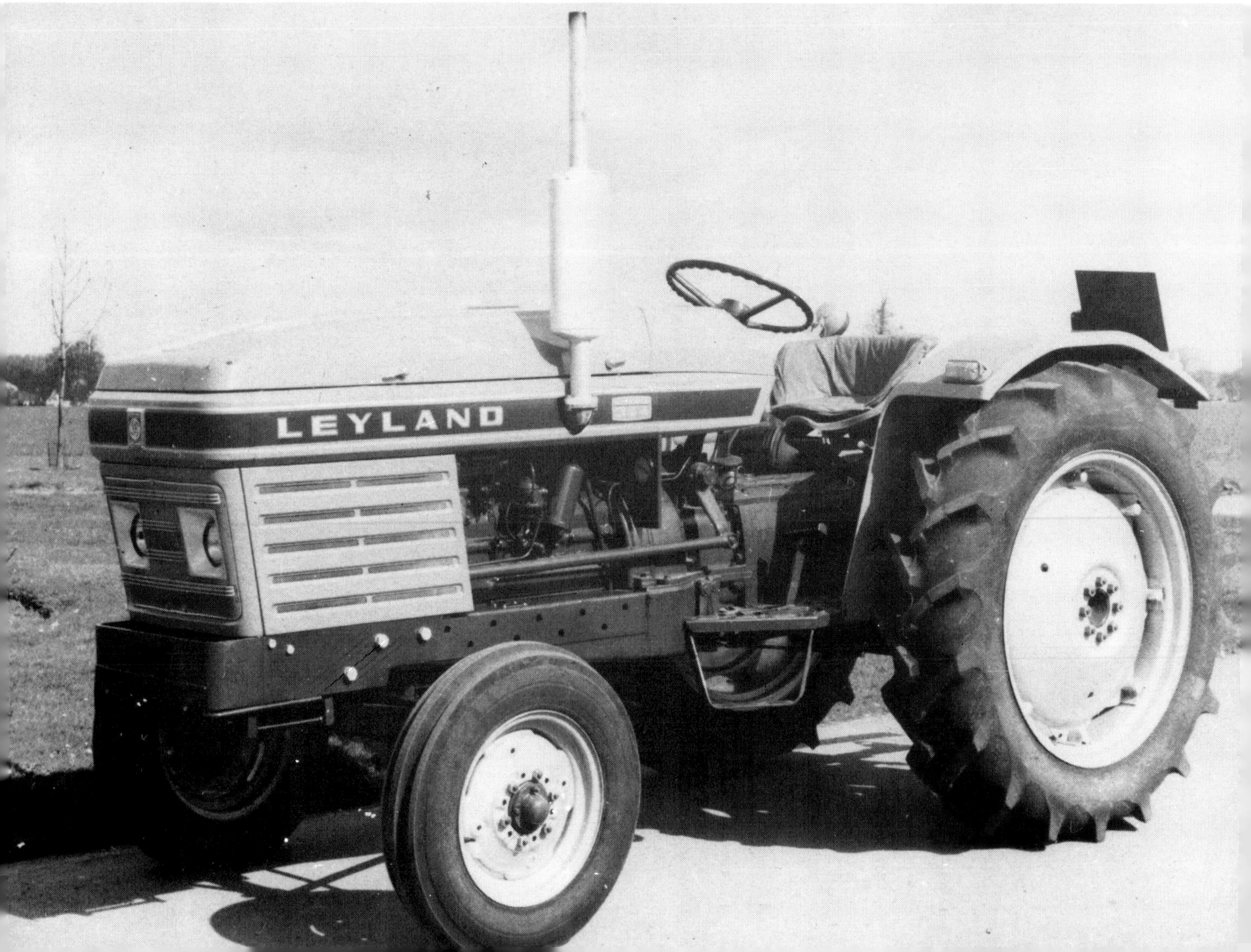
LEYLAND

At The Royal Show, in 1968, British Leyland stated its intention to consolidate and expand its tractor business from the plant at Bathgate. This modern production centre which had a capacity of 1000 tractors per week started manufacture of the BLUE RANGE of tractors in response to the dealers and farmers demands due to the loss of sales caused by the unpopular design of the 4/65 and 3/45 tractors. Introduced in November 1969 the new models were the 70HP 384 (opposite upper), the 55HP 344, and the 25HP 154. The Leyland tractors were little more than a repaint job with new tinwork however, except for the 344 which now had a four cylinder 3402cc engine. The successor to the 4/25 was the Leyland 154 and this had three cross bars added to the front grille and the Leyland colour scheme. Note the small NUFFIELD transfer above the model number (top). A high clearance version is seen above; later models were offered in petrol or diesel form, suitable for orchard, hop, or vineyard use.

Introduced in December 1971, the new 253 47hp used a Perkins 3-cylinder engine. Note lack of sideframes.

Below: The new 6-cylinder Leyland 285 featured a Leyland 6/98 engine. Introduced in 1973 it featured 'live' hydraulics, 2 speed PTO, wet brakes, and hydraulically operated clutch and brake systems.

Above: The Leyland 384 tractor with Bray 4WD conversion. This model was only in production for a year before being replaced by the last Bray Four 70.

Below: The Leyland 485 was the first 4WD model to be assembled completely at Bathgate.

The illustrations on this page show the 1975 272 model which was the 270 model uprated to 72hp with fuel system and pump changes. The top illustration shows a cabless tractor for export using 384 type mudguards, the centre shot shows an export canopy, and the lower shot a 'Q' cab, fitted for UK sale.

The 154 with new 1976 styling, ie silver bonnet stripe and new model transfers.

The 285 with 'Q' cab, introduced in 1976, showing white cab top and silver bonnet stripe.

Introduced in 1973 and improved throughout the years the 245 is seen here fitted with a Q cab and Synchro gearbox. Red stripes were added to the bonnet.

Above: The Leyland 262 fitted with front loader and SYNCHRO gearbox.

Below: Fitted with an assister ram, giving hydraulic lift of 5000lbs, the 482 had the engine power increased to 82HP from the previous 72HP unit, used in the 472 it succeeded in 1979.

The Leyland 4100 was the top of the range 100HP four wheel drive model. It was introduced in 1973.

Introduced in 1978 the 472 was 4WD version of the 272. The front axle was made by CARRIRO in Italy. This tractor is also fitted with the Leyland Synchro gearbox. This gave 9 forward and three reverse speeds.

In 1980, the new range of yellow and black tractors were introduced. The 245 became the 502; 262 the 602; 272 the 702; 472 the 704; 462 the 604; 282 the 802; 482 the 804; and the 235 was introduced as the 302 in mid 1981. The 235 was built in Turkey and had replaced the 154 in 1979 when UK production of this model ceased. The illustrations below show a selection of yellow models.

The 30HP 302, built in Turkey is seen above on ground maintenance duties whilst the Perkins engined 502 is seen below.

The 602 and 604 models shared the same 62HP Leyland 4/98DT engine; other features included fully live hydraulics, fully independent PTO, wet disc brakes and QM cab. The 604 is seen here.

The 700 series (the 702 is seen here) had a 72HP Leyland 4/98NT engine and the example here is fitted with the explorer cab.

The 800 series, exemplified by the 802 above and 804 below shared the
same 82HP turbocharged Leyland 4/98TT engine. The 600, 700 and 800 series all shared the same transmission layout.

Opposite page: 'Made better by Marshall' was the slogan in the new Marshall sales literature, now that the tractors were built at Gainsborough. They had
to pass on an 86-point check before leaving the factory. The 62HP 602 with QM cab is seen here in the top picture with QM cab, and the same model,
with deluxe explorer cab, in the centre shot. The 82HP 802 is seen in the bottom picture. Engines continued to be bought from Leyland and the 802 had
the 4/98 TT engine.

The Marshall 904 was powered by a 4-cylinder 92HP turbo-charged engine. This model later became the 904XL with creep speed transmission.

The new Marshall 100 series introduced in 1984. This model used the Leyland 6/98 6 cyl., engine which produced 103HP or 115HP in turbo-charged form. Note the famous Field Marshall emblem on the grille. The transmission for this model was imported from ZF in Germany.

Marshall tractors are now part of the Bentall Simplex group and are offered in 75, 85 and 95hp models, in either 2 or 4 wheel drive form, and to X or XL specification. All are fitted with Marshall Synchro transmission and are matched up to PERKINS power packs, with stronger rear axle differential. Compact tractors of 18hp and 26hp are also available based on Italian designs. The styling is exemplified by the 174 seen above. The range has since been extended and re-designed. Being current products, they are somewhat outwith the scope of this publication, but, in a future edition in years to come, they too, will no doubt, become history.

The 174 (above) was a one off, in fact the 100 series used the Leyland 6/98 series engine either naturally aspirated giving 103HP or Turbocharged, giving 115 HP, as used in the 115 below.

The Marshall 132 is in the 38-40HP bracket and features a three cylinder diesel engine, six forward and two reverse speeds, and is manufactured outwith the UK for Marshalls.

The 184 and 264 tractors are also made overseas for Marshall and feature aircooled diesel engines and are aimed at the estate market.